Black Men Can't Teach

A Collection of Black Male Voices

Kwashee Totimeh

First paperback edition April 2021

ISBN 978-0-578-90154-1 (paperback)

This book is dedicated to my unborn child.

I Love You.

Prologue:

My Educational Philosophy

Before we jump into what this book is and why it is titled *Black Men Can't Teach* I want to share my educational philosophy. An educational philosophy is a statement about your method of teaching and the values you would want to implement within your classroom. The following are my core values when it comes to education. These are the things I want to embody every time I step into the classroom and it's showtime.

Potential...

I believe that each and every child has the potential to achieve the unthinkable once they set their mind to it. As an educator, I believe that it is my responsibility to unlock this potential and push them beyond the surface to unleash their highest potential. I will help students to develop their potential by strongly believing in them, as I know the impact this can have on an individual from personal experience. Thinking back to my younger days as a student, I had only two teachers that believed in me and pushed me to be the best that I could be. This was such a motivation for my progress, hence why I feel strongly about this interaction with my students as well. I want to be the educator that shows up and supports my students, reassuring them that I believe in them and they can accomplish anything once they put in the time and work to do so.

Care...

*As an educator, students often spend
more time with us than their parents
during the school week. It is important to
not only assume the teaching role for
our students but also to genuinely
care about them and their well-being on
a daily basis. We must be understanding
and conversational, realizing the impact
we have on their lives. Every day I want
to ask my students how was their day
yesterday, what did they do and how are
they feeling? These questions show that I
care and remain engaged in their lives
beyond schoolwork. I was never asked
these questions during my school days as
it was often strictly learning, but the
reality is if a student feels that you
actually care, they are more willing to
learn. In turn, this creates a great
learning environment for your students
in and outside of the classroom.*

Creativity...

My personal goal for my classrooms is to challenge students and watch them blossom into their true full potential. In my classroom, I want students to have freedom of expression as well as creativity. It is very important to me to implement creativity in the classroom as students can be themselves and bring a new dynamic to our space. By finding creative spins to put on common lessons, I find that students are more excited and engaged. Opening them up to innovative ideas allows them to use critical thinking and push their limits to accomplish a goal.

I wrote this education philosophy in September of 2016 before I began teaching. This is what I envisioned bringing to my classrooms. This is the energy I wanted as every individual walked into my classroom. As I began my teaching career, I realized that it is a fight to establish these core values. This educational system makes it hard for an individual to teach from the heart. How can teachers be expected to implement creativity with only forty-five-minute prep periods to plan for six classes? I do my best to make sure students know I care and will push them to their truest potential. But within the educational system, you find it is nothing but a big game of politics, and with politics means you are sacrificing your morals.

Chapter 1: First Year of Teaching

If you picked up this book hoping to find all the reasons why black men are incapable of being teachers, I'm sorry to say; this ain't it.

This is a book to show you the importance of black male teachers for our students of color.

Now I know the title is misleading, but it made you pick this book up; so, it did its job. I chose this title because this is how many Black male educators feel at times teaching in America. This is the feeling we get after we are constantly shot down in meetings after we voice our opinion. When they assume we do not have the proper knowledge on how to handle students due to society's negative view of Black males. This is the feeling we receive when we are only shown importance when we are constantly called upon to handle a troubled student.

This is why I entitled this book *Black Men Can't Teach…* Now let's dive in.

I want to share a few facts with you just in case you were not aware before we dive into the lives of black male teachers in America.

.

Fact 1

According to the National Center for Education Statistics, there are around 3.1 million public school teachers total in the United States. An estimated two percent (60,000) of those teachers are black males.[i]

Fact 2

Black students exposed to one black teacher by third grade were thirteen percent more likely to enroll in college. Those who had two black teachers were thirty-two percent more likely to enroll in college. [ii]

Fact 3

Exposure to at least one black teacher in grades three to five also increases the likelihood that persistently low-income students of both sexes aspire to attend a four-year college.[iii]

I want to start this book off with
honesty. I never wanted to be a teacher. I
only became a teacher because it was the
one job that could help me pay off my
school loans at the time. I am glad it led
me to this decision; I would not change
it for the world. Becoming a New York
City teacher really developed me, and
the children helped me become the man
I am today. It was not that I only taught
these students; they taught me too.

Walking into education, my expectations of being a teacher versus the reality of being a teacher was very different. I expected that teaching would be a walk in the park. I would just have to look at a lesson that was already made, teach it to students, input grades, and enjoy three months of summer vacation. Well, that is not the role of the teacher. The first thing I learned is that every school is different, and not everyone is there to help you. You would've thought that everyone would be so helpful in a school building due to the main goal being the students' success. The reality is that you may be left on an island to figure things out on your own, and everyone will refuse the help you ask for.

Yes, there are rough times as a Black male educator. Times that will truly test you and break you, but it's an experience I wouldn't trade for the world. This experience made me a better man. It showed me what our youth are missing and that is positive male role models. I advise all Black men to teach in a school at one point in their life. This is a personal experience every Black male need in order to understand why they are needed as positive representations. Also, that one year of teaching can impact a student for the rest of their lives.

These are the situations I encountered as a first-year teacher. This is why I created this book. I wanted to highlight the importance of black male educators, our experiences, and why the numbers of black male teachers in America are low by sharing a collection of voices from black male educators.

__What was your experience in your first year of teaching?__

"There were a lot of teachers that were scolding me in a way. Like, Oh, you're supposed to do this and supposed to do that. It was very frustrating. It was rough; within like a month or two, I thought about leaving. But I stayed strong, and I just had to like ask questions. Some people were able to be helpful without scolding me or like belittling me. But, it was a balance of good and bad. It definitely made me stronger as a teacher."

-    28yo (Harlem, NY)

"I felt like I was prepared, and then when I first actually got into it, the first day I was like holy crap, this is not what I thought was going to be.

I had a lot of people in my corner as far as like support. But then I also had many people as far as like administration, that wasn't necessarily supporting us. It became, at some point, very overwhelming. It also came to the point where I was like frustrated, and I realized that education was more of a business and less geared toward helping.

I had a few teachers who definitely helped me and made it go by very easy per se. But it definitely would've been better if there was a better program or system."

\- 24 yo (Dover, DE)

"It was after my first year just getting out of college. It was a learning experience. I didn't know how to manage the classroom or how to create lesson plans. So that whole year was like a learning experience for me in terms of how to manage the kids, how to build a relationship with the kids, how to be yourself in a classroom, and how to be yourself in a system that's dominated by another race.

So, just learning how to navigate through that was very difficult. I did not have a good first year teaching, I had good moments, but I didn't have a good first year teaching."

-    24yo (Boston, MA)

"I think it was an experience that I wouldn't trade for the world. I learned a lot about teaching; I learned a lot about myself. That's the year that I think a lot of people decide if the profession is for them, not just if the school is for them. But I think if that profession is like what you want to do your first year, it could be traumatic in a way; it could be like some PTSD type-inducing thing. But I think if you look at the good and the bad, I think like there's always way more good than bad in your freshman year."

- 30yo (Brooklyn, NY)

"My first-year teaching was definitely one of my toughest experiences. It was tough, but it was also rewarding and a learning experience. I definitely went through a lot with learning how to plan lessons and learning how to build relationships with my students and also just things that may seem simple but aren't. Like, learning how to keep paper trails or take notes, email, and even professional duties. All those things were a learning experience that, you know, get knowledgeable about."

-    27yo (Bronx, NY)

"It was a lot of learning and lesson planning. A lot of what I realized later on was that there was unnecessary stuff that really wasn't benefiting the children. As far as lesson planning and pretests and post tests and test evaluations and standardized tests and things of that nature. There was a lot of professional development. That was kind of like a repeat of what you learned throughout college."

- 32yo (Lewes, DE)

"My first year of teaching was interesting. I felt like I was fighting the system, and I always called it the system because there was no other way for me to process it because I'm sitting here thinking to myself, there is no way. Like that, I have to use my time this way and say the language this way. It does not have to be the case. I felt like I could prove that didn't need to happen. Eventually, which I did."

- 25yo (Atlanta, GA)

Chapter 2: Views of the Educational System

After my first year of teaching, my views of the educational system were tainted. I realized that the educational system in America is a business, and the students are the product. Teaching in America is filled with politics within these schools. They say the students come first, but honestly, it seems the majority of everything is money-related and not for the students' benefit.

For the children's needs to be met, teacher's well-being needs to be of equal value. We cannot have administrators continuously saying, "We put the students first," but have your teachers overworked. How can a student succeed if the person who guides them (the teacher) runs on four hours of sleep due to grading papers and creating lesson plans for five classes? This is all due to the fact that a teacher has one prep period of forty-five minutes during a school period and has to use their time to actually prep for their remaining classes throughout the day and review the work of the classes they just left. How can a student succeed if the teacher has to find time in their day to put up a bulletin board because it has become a high order from admin? Let me answer these questions for you; these students cannot succeed.

Everything is data, data, data; there is more value in data than there is on students' and teachers' well-being. You are not seeing a lot of administrators having luncheons with students daily to stay updated on the students' lives and how they are learning.

I feel morals and emotions have been removed from the education system. Teachers are expected to throw their morals out the window and commit a disservice to these students over and over. This is why I see myself leaving the educational system soon if there is no change.

What were your views of the educational system in America after your first year of teaching?

"After my first year, I realized the educational system, as for high school students in Prince George's County public school system, is failing the students and not only by grade but also with students being college-ready. These students are not becoming college-ready. These students are enduring great manipulation. I have even been told to change grades which I have refused not to. Administration fails to identify the loophole because they are getting the numbers that they want, falsely at that."

- 26yo (Oakland, CA)

"I saw the disparity between what my students could have access to, like the programs and just general things they could do in the school. I noticed that there are strong limits on what students in predominantly urban neighborhoods are exposed to. A lot of the times, we hear the narrative that black kids only want to play basketball and be a rapper, so what does the educational system do. They have a music class.

So, I'm like, I mean, that's cool, but why don't we show them how to be business people? I mean, outside of just the one day of career day where they get to talk with somebody for like 40 minutes. I have an ongoing program where my students get to like learn about businesses and learn about financial literacy or learn about how to manage a band or how to actually build video games."

\-   29yo (Manhattan, NY)

"Education needs to be revamped. I felt like there needs to be more creative ways to approach teaching. Teaching should not look the same for everyone. I feel like you honestly can't just teach out of a textbook, meaning like people can't just say our teacher should look like this."

-     31yo (Washington, D.C.)

"I'm very pessimistic about the system. Working in inner city schools, you start to see they are pushing for numbers and butts in seats, but they're not being educated. I started to see that it was really a numbers game.

I also started to see how in some schools where you have a Teach for America or white individual that is not equipped to work in inner city schools. A lot of times they have what we sometimes call a God complex. They feel like they can come in and fix the kids, save the kids. A lot of these people are not in it for actually educating kids, as in the whole child. We are not talking just standing in front of them in the classroom and saying, one plus one is two. There are life skills that should be incorporated when we teach. We need individuals to expose these kids to different things."

- 24yo (Newark, NJ)

"After my first year, I wanted to quit. I called the person who referred me and told them that I don't want to make your name look bad, but I don't want to be here. It felt more like the kids were in prison and more in trouble all the time than they were ever praised. I couldn't get behind the idea of always looking for the wrong. I started to question myself and my integrity and like, was this the place for me? I started to question if I was altering my morals because I didn't agree with a lot of the things."

-    29yo (Brooklyn, NY)

Chapter 3: Red Flags

This chapter is to help everyone that is looking into teaching. When you are coming from a different profession or never majored in education, then teaching is unchartered waters.

I remember going into my first interview, which was my first and only. I was in my last week of the teacher training program and had like three months to find a school to be placed. This being all new to me, I was kind of in a panic. I related finding a job in the teaching realm to finding a job in corporate America. I thought it was going to be a hard task with many interviews and waiting on callbacks. So, every day I am on edge because this was my risk it all. I get invited to a school job fair…

So, fast forward through the job fair. I get invited by two schools to interview. School A wants to meet on Monday, and school B wants to meet on Thursday. Both of these schools are elementary/ middle schools combined. Monday arrives, and I attend school A's interview. When I walked in, it was very quiet and clean. The principal takes me on a tour of the school. He highlights so many good things about the school, their music program, friendly staff, high performance, etc. I am just eating all of this up, the tour ends, and we get back to his office. He asks me what I think, and next thing I know, he's asking me would I like to accept a position. Mind you, I didn't even have a demo lesson or ask any questions.

I tell him that I have another interview on Thursday and have to think about it. So, I leave the interview, and about thirty minutes later, I get a call from the principal again. He states that the offer is very time-sensitive, and they would need an answer that same day. So, I begin to panic because I'm thinking, what if I don't get another chance at a school hiring me. I frantically accept the position. As a young twenty-year-old with a heavy school loan, lacking knowledge of the teacher hiring process,

and just scared of not finding
somewhere, I made a decision.

The reason for this chapter is because I
made a mistake that I would want others
to avoid. When I entered that school for
my first day of work, it was not the place
that the principal had told me about or
showed me. I hope the voices of these
teachers will help to understand the
importance of not rushing. There are so
many schools looking for teachers, you
are very valuable and should find a
school that fits you. At the end of the
chapter, I will add questions for future
teachers to use to help them see those
red flags in their interviews.

What are some Red Flags when interviewing?

52

"The red flags that I would say is how the school is structured. If the school doesn't have proper structure, proper support, it's a red flag. I feel like a school should have a proper structure for teacher development and how to support the kids that are having behavior issues. Giving teachers support in managing their classroom."

- 24yo (Detroit, MI)

"Ask legitimate questions about what the workday is like and what administrators value. If you hear administrators talking more about logistics than the well-being of the students and staff, then it is clear what they prioritize. If you noticed that there's certain literature that's being prioritized rather than a holistic viewpoint, then that may not be the space for you. Find schools that really align with your own interests so that you can have that sense of work-life balance and the opportunity to recharge yourself. Teachers just coming into this profession needs to understand that they don't have to sacrifice themselves to be a good teacher."

-    34yo (Brooklyn, NY)

"This has actually happened with me when admin at a school blatantly tells you, this is probably a bit of a struggle, or you might want to interview at another place as well. Or they say, don't just immediately accept it or feel free to look elsewhere. That should be an immediate red flag where you ask yourself, why are they pushing me away so quickly. I think also having the right questions and knowing what to ask is important. Asking about the support system that they have for the kids. If the school doesn't clearly define what they have to support their students, then that's another red flag."

\-   25yo (Washington, D.C.)

"One big red flag for me is when the interviewer cannot answer important direct questions. I interviewed at a school, and I was asking them what their curriculum was for history. I was being interviewed to be a history teacher, and they were not answering any questions. He kept giving me the runaround, saying, "well, you know, we've talked about this, we talked about that." I said, okay, but what's your curriculum? They're not telling me what they are teaching the kids. When I asked very specific questions about historical events, they didn't really have an understanding of it; even the head of the history department didn't have an understanding of it."

- 27yo (Philadelphia, PA)

"I think most of my red flags involve administration across the board. When administration is poor, the students are poor. Another red flag is when the whole school administration is treating the school like a prison."

- 35yo (Charlotte, NC)

"To answer that question, I would say, what is the administration level of support and what is the actual trajectory of new teachers, how do they plan to support new teachers? What does that look like? How do they grow? How do they coach you? Do they listen when coaching?"

- 29yo (Los Angeles, CA)

"A red flag for me is how long has the leadership been there? Usually, I like to hear more than two years. Like if you've been there for about two years, I feel very comfortable. For myself it means you have a well-groomed team and have an understanding of the school and the dynamics and the nuances of the teachers. I also like asking to meet teachers in the school like impromptu. When the administration is protective about having conversation with teacher's impromptu that's also a red flag."

- 25yo (Queens, NY)

Questions to Ask During Your Interview

How does the school support students that are having behavior issues?

How does the school support teachers in managing classrooms?

Are there ways the school show appreciation to all cultures within the building?

Can you elaborate on the day-to-day responsibilities this job entails?

What are the administrators' values?

Do you have any other forms of supporting teachers?

What is the curriculum like for (insert subject you are applying for)?

How does the school support students who are not on their grade level for reading?

Are there any teachers available to speak with?

What is the administration's level of support?

How does the school support new teachers, and what does it look like?

What are the qualities you are looking for in this position?

What are some challenges you've seen people in this role encounter?

What learning resources are accessible for the students?

What opportunities does this school offer for professional growth?

How would you describe the students here?

Are there pre-made lesson plans? If so, do the teachers have to follow the lesson plan like a script, or can we add and remove as we see fit?

Chapter 4: For the Love of Teaching

What I love about teaching…

There are so many things I love about teaching. The most prominent thing I love is how these students have helped me to develop into a man. Teaching students that remind you of yourself will help you to build stronger connections to them. These stronger connections will help you to realize what you were missing as a child growing up. You will understand the importance of carrying yourself as a man and not as a child. I do not mean child as a person's age but as a mindset. I tell my students that they are young adults and deserve the respect as such. I truly believe to be a child is a mindset and not an age.

Our community is missing positive male role models that are not only athletic or musically-inclined. There are students in urban communities whose parents are not hands-on, or they don't even have a father in their lives. When you just listen to students, you understand what they are missing and what you are missing as an individual to impact your neighborhood positively.

Teaching in America helps to deepen your value of education. When I say education, I do not mean a school, I am referring to the value of learning. I value education today more than I ever did. I believe that we have to build connections with anything that we want a student to learn to something that is relatable to them. It's also important to show how those connections can apply to them in present day. Teaching makes you realize that a student won't care until they can understand what they are taught. Just because we tell them to do something, does not mean that they will value what they have done. We must always remember to educate is to lead to understanding.

Students tell me how they never have people putting faith in their abilities or building their confidence. I then think how growing up, I did not have this either, especially from my teachers. I always make sure to reassure students of their individual, unique, and amazing strengths. I want students to know we all have flaws, but we also all have strengths.

What do you Love Most About Teaching?

"I love the growth and the relationships that I build with the kids. I love the "aha I got it" moments and the "I didn't know that". I love when I build the relationship with the kids where we can have conversations about things outside of academics. I got into teaching because obviously I want a better generation than mine."

- 28yo (Miami, FL)

"I love the realness of it. I love the fact that I can be me, I feel like everyone has like an inner child and when you're around kids you can just be as pure as you want to be. You don't have to put up this facade or this front. You genuinely could just be whoever it is you want to be and genuinely enjoy seeing them smile with it. Also, my favorite part of teaching is being able to see the child changing right in front of you and knowing that your dedication that made that happen."

- 30yo (Woodbridge, VA)

"It's the representation for me. I didn't have any black teachers until I got to college. So being from the hood and now teaching in my neighborhood. It just means a lot."

- 28yo (Philadelphia, PA)

*"I love like the connections and like
being able to be who you are. I feel like
a lot of jobs, you can't be who you are. I
feel like in teaching, if you're not who
you really are then like you're not going
to have a good experience. I love
bringing who I am to the classroom and
having kids that look like me and them
be able to relate.*

*I look forward to seeing them every day,
like just seeing their personalities come
out or their personalities grow brings
me joy."*

\-   28yo (Brooklyn, NY)

"Showing the kids something different. I know when I was a student there will be people who will come through or different teachers that would look different than what we looked like. But to have someone who looks like you and comes from a similar place and has a similar background circumstances, it kind of changes the perspective. It allows them to see different avenues that they can take. I feel like I'm just that vessel right now. So just showing them something different and being that vessel for them to expand their horizons."

- 26yo (Baltimore, MD)

"I love that it showed me how important it is to be an advocate for others that can't advocate for themselves. There are students that are afraid to advocate for themselves due to the stigma of kids not knowing anything or having to be quiet and take what they get. I believe in teaching students to advocate for themselves because when they have to go out into the real world they will need the skill of speaking up for themselves when someone does them wrong."

-    31yo (Brooklyn, NY)

*"First and foremost, I love my students.
In my four years, I can't say it's been
easy. I can say I've built relationships
with the kids where it's like even if I felt
stressed out or felt like something wasn't
going my way. I knew I had to give them
everything and they would give me it
back and it pay forward. They remember
not only stuff I taught them in the
classroom, but stuff about life too."*

-    25yo (Philadelphia, PA)

Chapter 5: Obtain and Retain

Why I wanted to quit…

During my first three years teaching, as a black male, I felt unwelcomed at my first school. The more students showed they genuinely liked me, the more I noticed coworkers despised me. Of course, not every school employee is like this, but no one should walk into any education space in an urban environment and feel uneasy.

I felt I was disliked for being a black male. As mentioned in chapter one, I was the only black male teacher in this school, with only two black women teachers in a K-8 school. I would have good days where students are intrigued and connecting to the material. Within the same day, I would have a supervisor find a way to belittle me and criticize the way I teach.

The main reason I wanted to quit was because I felt my morals were challenged every day. It hurts having to go to a job where you see students of color belittled by some (not all) white teachers in the south Bronx. Hearing students tell you how much they dislike the teachers because they make them feel like they are not good at anything. It hurts voicing your opinion to a principal and vice-principal about how students feel and not be heard. It hurts being told to teach in a way that your students are not receptive to. It hurts looking at these students and seeing yourself in each one of them and feeling their pain.

I wanted to quit every day, but every day I came back. I wanted to continue to enjoy lunch with a class full of students talking about life and playing Super Smash Bros. on my Nintendo switch with them. I wanted to see the students I started with reach their finish line and graduate middle school.

One thing that could help obtain Black male educators is accountability. Nobody cares when a Black male educator leaves, but they always want to hire Black male educators. Nobody asks the right questions, like why are Black male educators leaving?
There is always a high push to get us into schools but there's never a push to

see why there are so many Black male educators leaving.

Now, if you are reading this, my time to quit is coming. I have run my course within the educational system in America. It's time for me to use the skills I have learned and the difficulties I've encountered to help heal and teach the community. One thing I want any individual that reads this book to do is ask themselves "How can I help?".

This chapter was developed for schools to notice the low number of black male educators and why they leave.

How to obtain Black male educators?

"I know this may sound disparaging, but first thing I would do is actually lower the standards and the criteria for becoming a teacher in general because it's not even just black male teachers, like teachers in general. It's hard to recruit people. The other thing I would say is I would want a place where we are not seen as a source of entertainment. Like the only two times I ever really see black men in the news is if we do something super cool, like, Oh, they started a rap group or when they taught their kids how to do handshakes."

- 30yo (Harlem, NY)

"I would say not looking at us as like the trophy. I think that at times the black male teacher is viewed in that way, like they always say, "Oh well, you know, we have this, you all do this." I will also say, start with the fact that you're able to build a community within a community, which allows them to let their creativity shine. Allow the hiring process to show what kind of change they want to bring versus what kind of thing that you want them to do. Allow them to see that teaching is not just dreadful. It's actually a fun career to do, if it's done right."

- 27yo (Chicago, IL)

"We have to change our idea of the profession. Even in the African American culture, teaching isn't looked at as a male profession. Parents tell us that you have to be a doctor, lawyer, engineer, or businessman. They never say a teacher because there's no money or value in it. I can't go to grandma's 50th birthday party and be like, my son is a teacher now and get that same respect if my son was a doctor or whatever. Our idea of being a teacher is like a job that's less than."

- 25yo (Queens, NY)

*"Adequately compensate teachers, you
know what I'm saying? Give real
positions and treat us with respect and
in meaningful ways. Like listen to us."*

-   28yo (Philadelphia, PA)

"I think a lot of problems with not having enough black male teachers is the advertisement of the profession. Most people would think teaching is a female job, when it's really not. There's a sense of, it's a soft job and you can't be powerful masculine and be in front of a class. But that's exactly what our students need to see . They need to see a powerful masculine person who can be soft and can be caring and be nurturing in front of the class. Someone who looks like them, to challenge those stereotypes."

- 27yo (Paterson, NJ)

How to keep Black Male Educators?

"Experiencing bullying from administration and lack of support, in my perspective are the two main reasons why Black Male Educators are leaving the profession. Bullying is a very common tactic administration and teachers use when trying to eliminate Black Male Educators from the school. The majority of Non-Black educators believe that Black Male Educators are receiving too much attention from the students, which causes conflict between the Non-Black Educators and the Black Male Educators in the building.

Lack of support is another reason as to why Black Male Educators leave the profession. Black Male Educators, if employed in a majority Non-Black

86

faculty, they will be placed in a classroom with limited resources they have to use to impact their students' learning. They will usually not receive the same amount of gratitude as their Non-Black colleagues who, when entering into the school building, will receive help from the administration. Instead, Black Male Educators will be expected to over-perform with the very little materials given to them by the administration."

-    30yo (Hartford, CT)

"There is no fulfillment in the field, and no sense of belonging. Education is a business, and many Black Men feel as though if they cannot be authentic in the educational spaces then they should not be there. Also economic disparities cause many Black Male educators to leave the education space because there isn't enough funding in academia."

-   26yo (Houston, TX)

"The main issue is that when Black Males enter the field they are really seen as what has been described to me as "Knuckle Draggers," or their sole purpose is for discipline within schools. They are not pushed to pursue curriculum endeavors for growth and content building. The first thing they want Black Males to do is control the children of color which is why most are pushed to serve in the roles of "Dean of Discipline". This in turn may have them to feel like they are only being used for their body and presence and nothing else. It really points to the lack of support and career development."

- 26yo (Baltimore, MD)

"Hmm… I know for me personally is treat my degree and my skill set with some kind of dignity."

-    26yo (Richmond, VA)

"I think when a black male teacher gets into the system of education, allowing that black male teacher to be themselves is important. To create their own classroom, to make their own safe environment and to be themselves. To have a voice in the climate of the school and the environment of the school. Also, promote opportunities for more educational growth, as far as if that black man wants to further his education. To have scholarships available for the younger man who graduated from high school and wants to pursue teaching but can't afford it or wants to pursue a career but can't afford it because of the expense of college."

- 28yo (Chicago, IL)

"The way to keep black male teachers is to bring in more black male teachers. I can speak for myself that I would say my best resource has been other black male educators. That is why I stayed, being able to have somebody to talk to and somebody that could understand what my experience is from my lens and not trying to minimize my feelings if I'm feeling negative. Someone who can emphasize my experience when I'm feeling positive about things. Also, if these schools learn how to respect the humanity that black male teachers bring into schools, that can in turn bring more black male teachers in."

-   29yo (Camden, NJ)

"The schools have to take these exit interviews serious and really listen to what people will say. Sometimes it's a supervisor or the school culture. Sometimes there isn't the right support. So, they got to take the exit interview serious and really think about why people are leaving? And then just make specific strategic efforts to keep people in."

-    31yo (Washington, D.C.)

"I feel like they should make black male educators feel more welcomed. They should also put them in better positions where they can be leaders instead of just being in the background. Of course you have to be responsible enough to be able to take on that role. But I feel like there should be way more opportunities. Also, have those opportunities allow them to be able to grow within their field. I feel like in order for you to see what a person would do, you should be able to give them the opportunity to prove that."

- 29yo (Staten Island, NY)

"I believe Black Male educators are leaving for several reasons, one being that we are only used for classroom management positions and not given the opportunity to work in leadership, lack of Financial resources, and history is being taught to scholars from a white perspective. I myself left education altogether this past January and I have never felt any better. Not having to answer to anyone or report to a white leadership team member, and most of all not having to be micro managed as I watch my white colleagues do what they please."

-   28yo (Atlanta, GA)

Chapter 6: Twitter's Importance of Black Male Educators

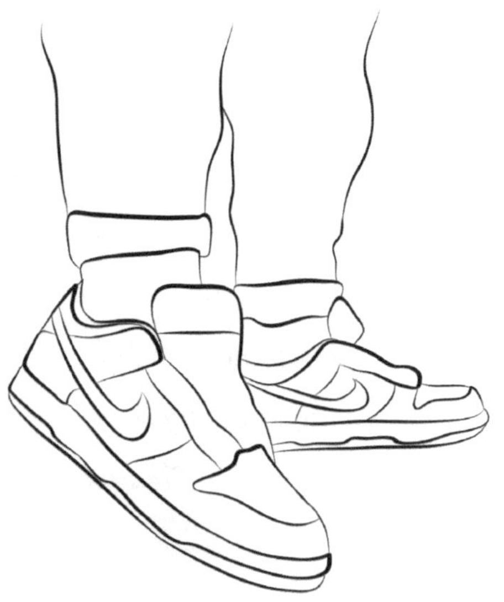

"When passionate and in a role, that's not gym or admin they're interactions are invaluable. A few of my favorite teachers was a black male. Each had a lot more patience for POC students than other teachers. They also almost always took the time to know people's parents/backgrounds."

- Anonymous Twitter User

"It's something that we don't see enough of. Every time I had a Black Male teacher they had profound impact on my life. Now as an educator, I try to pay it forward."

- Anonymous Twitter User

"Our youth need stronger black male representation."

- Anonymous Twitter User

"They don't take bs or any disrespect which is fire because it's humbling and validating. They're very accepting. They also are observant, inclusive, involved and pushes everyone to do their best. They all have a "no kid left behind" mentality from what I've experienced and that's SUCH an important mindset to have in a classroom because all kids learn and process material differently."

\-   Anonymous Twitter User

"We need more! it's amazing how much more the black boys in my class listen to a black male teacher than they do to black female teachers. I'm not even offended by it but a sometimes they need a strong male in their lives to teach them the things that I cannot as a black woman. I just wish more black men went into the teaching field because it is definitely a female dominated career."

- Anonymous Twitter User

"There aren't enough and it's unfortunate. The teacher's adult meet in their life affect their long-term view of the world as adults. Especially for black children. I hope I have the resources to ensure my children will have some black educators."

- Anonymous Twitter User

"I think we need more black male elementary school teachers. I work in a community school in the BX and we only have 2 black male teachers and 2 black male paras and when I say the students LOVE them especially the boys they relate to the paras OD."

- Anonymous Twitter User

"I think it mirrors how much black children need black men, in general. From my experience, black male teachers are usually respected and held as high authority figures. Black boys, specifically, feel like they have someone to look up to and connect with."

- Anonymous Twitter User

"It impacts all students in a major way. It changes the narrative of what they believe black men should be or strive for. I've also noticed that male teachers (in general), have greater success with classroom management. Overall, we need more black male teachers in our schools!!"

- Anonymous Twitter User

"Seeing Black men in positive roles is important. Black students and non-Black students get to see an alternative to the negative ways they are portrayed. Most of the Black male teachers I had were a balance of paternal and brotherly. This gave them the ability to connect on a different level and offer guidance directly from their own experiences. I've seen a lot of Black boys make positive decisions because of this."

- Anonymous Twitter User

"I had Black male teachers in high school, Chemistry and English. They gave me space to be myself, pep talks when I felt like trash, encouraged me to write and to think critically about the world around me."

- Anonymous Twitter User

"Mr. Jennings one of those teachers the whole hood knows because he took on roles beyond teaching. He allowed for imagination in the classroom but always kept it real. & if I saw him on the street today, he'd still remember me."

- Anonymous Twitter User

"My first black male teacher was Monterio in AFAM studies. He made me feel like I belonged at Temple and helped me be a better student."

\-   Anonymous Twitter User

"My Economics my senior year teacher in high school Mr. Farris. I wanted to be just like him."

\-   Anonymous Twitter User

"Only one until college. Mr. White, he was like my dad in middle school/early high school. We talked rap, girls, marriage, Black history, discipline, everything."

- Anonymous Twitter User

"I loved Mr. Starling he was my first black male teacher. He taught math. A subject that was not my best. No matter what he was the only teacher who made learning math fun and offered tutoring and extra credit for struggling students."

- Anonymous Twitter User

"Never been good with authority so I usually got in trouble for talking back. One teacher let me go off. He didn't react. After class, he said "what are you really angry about?" That conversation lead to my grades going up."

- Anonymous Twitter User

Epilogue: Words of Advice

Be Vulnerable

As black men, we need to show the students we are human. Tell the students your flaws as a student yourself. This allows students to see themselves in you, to see that they too can overcome whatever inner battles they may be going through. I personally do not believe in having to feel like I have power or authority over students. I do not want students to get a sense of "I'm better than you". I want students to know I was you and I am still you. We are all students to life no matter what stage of life.

Be yourself

Students can feel when you are not being your authentic self. Bring who you are to the table and not who you THINK they want to see. Being your authentic self helps you when it comes to delivering your lesson. You will find what works for you and your students when you are yourself. You have to be comfortable in your house for someone to believe it is yours.

References

[i] Kena, G., Hussar W., McFarland J., de Brey C., Musu-Gillette, L., et al. (2016). *The condition of education 2016* (NCES 2016-144). Washington, DC: U.S. Department of Education, National Center for Education Statistics.

[ii] Rosen, J. (2018, November 12). *Black students who have one black teacher are more likely to go to college*. The Hub.

[iii] Gershenson, S., M. D. Hart, C., Lindsay, C., & Papageorge, N. (2017, March). *The Long-Run Impacts of Same-Race Teachers*. Iza.

www.ingramcontent.com/pod-product-compliance
Lightning Source LLC
Chambersburg PA
CBHW031350060726
47590CB00007B/2708